KEEP CALM

AND

CUDDLE UP

For Sharon

KEEP CALM AND CUDDLE UP

GOOD ADVICE FOR THOSE IN LOVE

EBURY
PRESS

5 7 9 10 8 6 4

First published in 2012 by Ebury Press, an imprint of Ebury Publishing
A Random House Group company

Copyright © Ebury Press 2012

The Random House Group Limited Reg. No. 954009

Addresses for companies within
The Penguin Random House Group can be found at:
global.penguinrandomhouse.com

A CIP catalogue record for this book is available
from the British Library

Penguin Random House is committed to a sustainable future for
our business, our readers and our planet. This book is made from
Forest Stewardship Council® certified paper.

Printed and bound in Great Britain by Clays Ltd, Elcograf S.p.A.

ISBN 9781785039706

To buy books by your favourite authors and register for offers visit
www.randomhouse.co.uk

WHAT THE WORLD REALLY NEEDS IS MORE LOVE AND LESS PAPER WORK.

Pearl Bailey

CONTENTS

Your cheating heart

Breaking up

The ex factor

Finding 'the one'

Love is …

Lovers' tiff

Suspicious minds

The real thing

Proposing

Like a horse and carriage

Keep the flame burning

Valentine

Birds do it, bees do it

Love is blind

Romance

INTRODUCTION

What is it about love? Songs have been composed, poems written, wars waged and lips split outside nightclubs because of it. The image of the lover is everywhere – indeed, so familiar have a few of these become that they now operate as a kind of cultural shorthand. Want to quickly show the pain of first love? Then how about a bobbysocked teenager weeping into her pillow. What about the impetuous spontaneity of youthful romance? Surely a peppy young buck, guitar strapped to his back climbing a vine to an open window.

When considering the fate of famous lovers, it's surprising that anyone goes in for it, really. Paris and Helen of Troy hooked up, only for his home town to get pillaged and burned by her jealous ex. Anthony and Cleopatra ended badly; a nasty business involving snakes. And Romeo and Juliet are enough to put anyone off for life. Every soap opera depends upon the love triangle, the thwarted desire, the forbidden love. The course of true love can never run smooth. But, and here's the odd thing, this is what we *want*. We don't actually like to see people fall happily in love and stay that way – what we prefer is for the blissful couple to be rent apart by infidelity with a randy greengrocer, or psychologically destroyed by a bitter ex who has returned to wreak havoc in paradise.

But of course, in real life, what we want is proper, true love. The search for love can lead us to some strange places, and new frontiers, but it also relies on the mundane, too. How many people met the person they love through work, for instance? Or through school or college? Or through their friends? The Venn diagrams of our lives mean that we are far more likely to meet 'the one' over the photocopier than we are when we happen to be out dragon slaying.

The newest frontier of course is the internet. Internet dating is big, big business because it works. It might seem an unnatural way to meet people, but really, is it any more of a manufactured way of meeting people than the dances and balls and formal social events of previous ages? The unique angle of internet dating, though, is potentially it allows anyone to meet *anyone*. Suddenly the pool we can fish in for a potential mate is vast. The opportunities are unlimited. But even this newest form of meeting people is still underpinned by the oldest desire – to love and be loved. St Valentine isn't likely to become the patron saint of broadband any time soon.

So enjoy this collection of lovingly selected quotes, assembled to keep the flame in your heart burning bright. In tough times when everything else becomes uncertain, there is still love. So, go on, *Keep Calm and Cuddle Up*.

ATTRACTION

EVERYONE SAYS THAT LOOKS DON'T MATTER, AGE DOESN'T MATTER, MONEY DOESN'T MATTER. BUT I NEVER MET A GIRL YET WHO HAS FALLEN IN LOVE WITH AN OLD UGLY MAN WHO'S BROKE.

Rodney Dangerfield

THE AVERAGE MAN IS MORE INTERESTED IN A WOMAN WHO IS INTERESTED IN HIM THAN HE IS IN A WOMAN WITH BEAUTIFUL LEGS.

Marlene Dietrich

THE WAY TO A WOMAN'S HEART IS THROUGH YOUR WALLET.

Frank Dane

**I BELIEVE THAT
IT'S BETTER TO
BE LOOKED OVER
THAN IT IS TO BE
OVERLOOKED.**

Mae West

**SCIENTISTS NOW
BELIEVE THAT
THE PRIMARY
BIOLOGICAL
FUNCTION OF
BREASTS IS TO
MAKE MALES
STUPID.**

Dave Barry

A CLEVER, UGLY MAN EVERY NOW AND THEN IS SUCCESSFUL WITH THE LADIES, BUT A HANDSOME FOOL IS IRRESISTIBLE.

William Makepeace Thackeray

**LUST FADES, SO
YOU'D BETTER BE
WITH SOMEONE WHO
CAN STAND YOU.**

Alan Zweibel

FLIRTING

FLIRTATION: ATTENTION WITHOUT INTENTION.

Paul Blouet

**TO AVOID MISTAKES
AND REGRETS,
ALWAYS CONSULT
YOUR WIFE BEFORE
ENGAGING IN A
FLIRTATION.**

E W Howe

A BEAUTY IS A WOMAN YOU NOTICE; A CHARMER IS ONE WHO NOTICES YOU.

Adlai Stevenson II

WHY DOES A
MAN TAKE IT FOR
GRANTED THAT A
GIRL WHO FLIRTS
WITH HIM WANTS HIM
TO KISS HER – WHEN,
NINE TIMES OUT
OF TEN, SHE ONLY
WANTS HIM TO WANT
TO KISS HER?

Helen Rowland

**FLIRTING IS THE SIN
OF THE VIRTUOUS
AND THE VIRTUE
OF THE SINFUL.**

Paul Bourget

SEDUCTION

A WOMAN'S CHASTITY CONSISTS, LIKE AN ONION, OF A SERIES OF COATS.

Nathaniel Hawthorne

**THE RESISTANCE
OF A WOMAN TO
A MAN'S ADVANCES
IS NOT ALWAYS A
SIGN OF VIRTUE.
SOMETIMES IT'S
JUST A SIGN OF
EXPERIENCE.**

Ninon de Lenclos

THE ART OF LOVE ... IS LARGELY THE ART OF PERSISTENCE.

Albert Ellis

A GENTLEMAN
IS SIMPLY A
PATIENT WOLF.

Lana Turner

A GENTLEMAN DOESN'T POUNCE, HE GLIDES.

Quentin Crisp

DATING

**DATING IS
PRESSURE AND
TENSION. WHAT IS
A DATE, REALLY,
BUT A JOB
INTERVIEW THAT
LASTS ALL NIGHT?**

Jerry Seinfeld

ODDS ON MEETING A SINGLE MAN: 1 IN 23; A CUTE, SINGLE MAN: 1 IN 429; A CUTE, SINGLE, SMART MAN: 1 IN 3,245,873; WHEN YOU LOOK YOUR BEST: 1 IN A BILLION.

Lorna Adler

WATCHING YOUR DAUGHTER BEING COLLECTED BY HER DATE FEELS LIKE HANDING OVER A MILLION DOLLAR STRADIVARIUS TO A GORILLA.

Jim Bishop

**EMPLOYEES MAKE
THE BEST DATES.
YOU DON'T HAVE TO
PICK THEM UP AND
THEY'RE ALWAYS
TAX-DEDUCTIBLE.**

Andy Warhol

**MY FATHER TOLD
ME ALL ABOUT THE
BIRDS AND THE BEES,
THE LIAR – I WENT
STEADY WITH A
WOODPECKER TILL
I WAS TWENTY-ONE.**

Bob Hope

(COMPUTER DATING) IT'S TERRIFIC IF YOU'RE A COMPUTER.

Rita Mae Brown

**A MAN CAN
SLEEP AROUND NO
QUESTIONS ASKED,
BUT IF A WOMAN
MAKES 19 OR 20
MISTAKES, SHE'S
A TRAMP.**

Joan Rivers

UNREQUITED
LOVE

**LET NO ONE WHO
LOVES BE CALLED
UNHAPPY. EVEN LOVE
UNRETURNED HAS
ITS RAINBOW.**

J M Barrie

**NOTHING TAKES
THE TASTE OUT OF
PEANUT BUTTER
QUITE LIKE
UNREQUITED
LOVE.**

Charlie Brown

PERHAPS A GREAT LOVE IS NEVER RETURNED.

Dag Hammarskjöld

SYMPTOMS
OF LOVE

LOVE IS LIKE AN HOURGLASS, WITH THE HEART FILLING UP AS THE BRAIN EMPTIES.

Jules Renard

LOVE IS LIKE THE MEASLES, ALL THE WORSE WHEN IT COMES LATE.

Mary Roberts Rinehart

ROMANTIC LOVE IS MENTAL ILLNESS. BUT IT'S A PLEASURABLE ONE. IT'S A DRUG. IT DISTORTS REALITY, AND THAT'S THE POINT OF IT. IT WOULD BE IMPOSSIBLE TO FALL IN LOVE WITH SOMEONE THAT YOU REALLY SAW.

Fran Lebowitz

**LOVE – A WILDLY
MISUNDERSTOOD
ALTHOUGH HIGHLY
DESIRABLE MALFUNCTION
OF THE HEART WHICH
WEAKENS THE BRAIN,
CAUSES EYES TO
SPARKLE, CHEEKS TO
GLOW, BLOOD PRESSURE
TO RISE AND THE LIPS
TO PUCKER.**

Anon

FIRST LOVE

**EVERY MAN IS
THOROUGHLY HAPPY
TWICE IN HIS LIFE:
JUST AFTER HE HAS
MET HIS FIRST LOVE,
AND JUST AFTER
HE HAS LEFT HIS
LAST ONE.**

H L Mencken

IT IS EASIER TO GUARD A SACK FULL OF FLEAS THAN A GIRL IN LOVE.

Yiddish proverb

ONE IS VERY CRAZY
WHEN IN LOVE.

Freud

**MEN ALWAYS WANT
TO BE A WOMAN'S
FIRST LOVE. WOMEN
HAVE A MORE
SUBTLE INSTINCT:
WHAT THEY LIKE
IS TO BE A MAN'S
LAST ROMANCE.**

Oscar Wilde

**BOYS WILL BE BOYS.
AND EVEN THAT
WOULDN'T MATTER
IF ONLY WE COULD
PREVENT GIRLS
FROM BEING GIRLS.**

Anthony Hawkins

LOVE MAKES THE TIME PASS. TIME MAKES LOVE PASS.

Euripides

**HOW ON EARTH
ARE YOU EVER
GOING TO EXPLAIN
IN TERMS OF
CHEMISTRY AND
PHYSICS SO
IMPORTANT A
BIOLOGICAL
PHENOMENON AS
FIRST LOVE?**

Einstein

KISSES AND CUDDLES

ALWAYS REMEMBER THIS: 'A KISS WILL NEVER MISS, AND AFTER MANY KISSES A MISS BECOMES A MISSES'.

John Lennon

A KISS IS A LOVELY TRICK DESIGNED BY NATURE TO STOP SPEECH WHEN WORDS BECOME SUPERFLUOUS.

Ingrid Bergman

IF YOU ARE EVER
IN DOUBT AS TO
WHETHER TO KISS
A PRETTY GIRL,
ALWAYS GIVE HER
THE BENEFIT OF
THE DOUBT.

Thomas Carlyle

A KISS CAN BE A COMMA, A QUESTION MARK OR AN EXCLAMATION POINT. THAT'S BASIC SPELLING THAT EVERY WOMAN OUGHT TO KNOW.

Mistinguett

IT TAKES A LOT OF EXPERIENCE FOR A GIRL TO KISS LIKE A BEGINNER.

Ladies Home Journal, 1948

YOUR
CHEATING
HEART

**IF YOU MARRY A
MAN WHO CHEATS
ON HIS WIFE, YOU'LL
BE MARRIED TO A
MAN WHO CHEATS
ON HIS WIFE.**

Ann Landers

**A CODE
OF HONOUR:
NEVER APPROACH
A FRIEND'S
GIRLFRIEND
OR WIFE WITH
MISCHIEF AS YOUR
GOAL. THERE ARE
JUST TOO MANY
WOMEN IN THE
WORLD TO JUSTIFY**

THAT SORT OF DISHONOURABLE BEHAVIOUR. UNLESS SHE'S REALLY ATTRACTIVE.

Bruce Jay Friedman

IT IS BETTER TO BE UNFAITHFUL THAN TO BE FAITHFUL WITHOUT WANTING TO BE.

Brigitte Bardot

**MY ATTITUDE
TOWARD MEN WHO
MESS AROUND IS
SIMPLE: IF YOU FIND
'EM, KILL 'EM.**

Loretta Lynn

**NO LOVER, IF HE BE
OF GOOD FAITH, AND
SINCERE, WILL DENY
HE WOULD PREFER
TO SEE HIS MISTRESS
DEAD THAN
UNFAITHFUL.**

Marquis de Sade

**EVERY MAN NEEDS
TWO WOMEN: A
QUIET HOME-MAKER,
AND A THRILLING
NYMPH.**

Iris Murdoch

ALL IS FAIR IN LOVE AND WAR.

Edward Smedley

BREAKING
UP

DON'T CRY FOR A MAN WHO'S LEFT YOU, THE NEXT ONE MAY FALL FOR YOUR SMILE.

Mae West

**DON'T CRY
BECAUSE IT'S OVER.
SMILE BECAUSE IT
HAPPENED.**

Dr Seuss

**POSSIBLY THE WORST
BREAK UP LINE EVER:
IT'S NOT ME, IT'S YOU.**

Anon

DON'T WASTE TIME
TRYING TO BREAK A
MAN'S HEART; BE
SATISFIED IF YOU
CAN JUST MANAGE
TO CHIP IT IN A
BRAND NEW PLACE.

Helen Rowland

THE HEART WAS
MADE TO BE BROKEN.

Oscar Wilde

IT IS FOOLISH TO TEAR ONE'S HAIR IN GRIEF, AS THOUGH SORROW WOULD BE MADE LESS BY BALDNESS.

Cicero

THE HOTTEST LOVE HAS THE COLDEST END.

Socrates

FRIENDSHIP IS CERTAINLY THE FINEST BALM FOR THE PANGS OF DISAPPOINTED LOVE.

Jane Austen

IN THE ARITHMETIC
OF LOVE, ONE PLUS
ONE EQUALS
EVERYTHING, AND
TWO MINUS ONE
EQUALS NOTHING.

Mignon McLaughlin

THE EX
FACTOR

SCRATCH A LOVER,
AND FIND A FOE.

Dorothy Parker

A WOMAN'S DESIRE FOR REVENGE OUTLASTS ALL HER OTHER EMOTIONS.

Cyril Connolly

LOOKING GOOD IS
THE BEST REVENGE.

Ivana Trump

IS THERE A CURE FOR
A BROKEN HEART?
ONLY TIME CAN HEAL
YOUR BROKEN
HEART, JUST AS
TIME CAN HEAL HIS
BROKEN ARMS
AND LEGS.

Miss Piggy

FINDING
'THE ONE'

WOMEN DESIRE SIX THINGS: THEY WANT THEIR HUSBANDS TO BE BRAVE, WISE, RICH, GENEROUS, OBEDIENT TO WIFE, AND LIVELY IN BED.

Chaucer

WHEN YOU LOVE SOMEONE ALL YOUR SAVED-UP WISHES START COMING OUT.

Elizabeth Bowen

BETTER TO HAVE LOVED A SHORT MAN THAN NEVER TO HAVE LOVED A TALL.

David Chambless

PUT YOUR HAND
ON A STOVE FOR
A MINUTE AND IT
SEEMS LIKE AN HOUR.
SIT WITH THAT
SPECIAL GIRL FOR AN
HOUR AND IT SEEMS
LIKE A MINUTE.
THAT'S RELATIVITY.

Einstein

LOVE IS ...

**LOVE IS SAYING
'I FEEL DIFFERENTLY'
INSTEAD OF
'YOU'RE WRONG'.**

Anon

THREE GRAND ESSENTIALS TO HAPPINESS IN THIS LIFE ARE SOMETHING TO DO, SOMETHING TO LOVE, AND SOMETHING TO HOPE FOR.

Joseph Addison

TRUE LOVE IS LIKE GHOSTS, WHICH EVERYBODY TALKS ABOUT AND FEW HAVE SEEN.

François, Duc de La Rochefoucauld

**ONE WORD FREES US
OF ALL THE WEIGHT
AND PAIN OF LIFE:
THAT WORD IS LOVE.**

Sophocles

**LET YOUR LOVE
BE LIKE THE MISTY
RAINS, COMING
SOFTLY, BUT
FLOODING
THE RIVER.**

Proverb

**LOVE IS A FIRE.
BUT WHETHER IT IS
GOING TO WARM
YOUR HEARTH OR
BURN DOWN YOUR
HOUSE, YOU CAN
NEVER TELL.**

Joan Crawford

LOVE IS AN OCEAN OF EMOTIONS ENTIRELY SURROUNDED BY EXPENSES.

Lord Dewar

LOVE IS METAPHYSICAL GRAVITY.

R Buckminster Fuller

LOVERS' TIFF

SILENCE IS ONE OF THE HARDEST ARGUMENTS TO REFUTE.

Josh Billings

NEVER GO TO
BED MAD. STAY UP
AND FIGHT.

Phyllis Diller

**ONCE A WOMAN
HAS FORGIVEN HER
MAN, SHE MUST NOT
REHEAT HIS SINS
FOR BREAKFAST.**

Marlene Dietrich

THE COURSE OF TRUE LOVE NEVER DID RUN SMOOTH.

Shakespeare

SUSPICIOUS
MINDS

**WHEN A HUSBAND
BRINGS HIS WIFE
FLOWERS FOR NO
REASON, THERE'S
A REASON.**

Molly McGee

**JEALOUSY IS
ALL THE FUN YOU
THINK THEY HAD.**

Erica Jong

MEN ARE ONLY AS LOYAL AS THEIR OPTIONS.

Bill Maher

THE REAL
THING

ANYONE CAN BE PASSIONATE, BUT IT TAKES REAL LOVERS TO BE SILLY.

Rose Franken

**TRUE LOVE IS LIKE
A PAIR OF SOCKS:
YOU GOTTA HAVE
TWO AND THEY'VE
GOTTA MATCH.**

Anon

MOST PEOPLE WOULD RATHER GIVE THAN GET AFFECTION.

Aristotle

WE DON'T BELIEVE IN RHEUMATISM AND TRUE LOVE UNTIL AFTER THE FIRST ATTACK.

Marie von Ebner-Eschenbach

IF LOVE IS THE ANSWER, COULD YOU PLEASE REPHRASE THE QUESTION?

Lily Tomlin

IN A GREAT ROMANCE, EACH PERSON BASICALLY PLAYS A PART THAT THE OTHER REALLY LIKES.

Elizabeth Ashley

IN OUR LIFE THERE IS
A SINGLE COLOUR,
AS ON AN ARTIST'S
PALETTE, WHICH
PROVIDES THE
MEANING OF LIFE
AND ART. IT IS THE
COLOUR OF LOVE.

Marc Chagall

LOVE WON'T BE
TAMPERED WITH,
LOVE WON'T GO
AWAY. PUSH IT TO
ONE SIDE AND
IT CREEPS TO
THE OTHER.

Louise Erdich

PROPOSING

THE SUREST WAY TO HIT A WOMAN'S HEART IS TO TAKE AIM KNEELING.

Douglas William Jerrold

MAN PROPOSES, WOMAN FORECLOSES.

Minna Antrim

LIKE A
HORSE AND
CARRIAGE

**BRIDE. A WOMAN
WITH A FINE
PROSPECT OF
HAPPINESS
BEHIND HER.**

Ambrose Bierce

MARRIAGE IS MORE THAN FOUR BARE LEGS IN A BED.

Hoshang N Akhtar

**NEVER MARRY A
MAN WHO HATES HIS
MOTHER, BECAUSE
HE'LL END UP
HATING YOU.**

Jill Bennett

**BEFORE MARRIAGE
A MAN YEARNS
FOR A WOMAN.
AFTERWARD THE
'Y' IS SILENT.**

W A Clarke

**WHATEVER YOU MAY
LOOK LIKE, MARRY
A MAN YOUR OWN
AGE – AS YOUR
BEAUTY FADES,
SO WILL HIS
EYESIGHT.**

Phyllis Diller

HAPPINESS IN MARRIAGE IS ENTIRELY A MATTER OF CHANCE.

Jane Austen

I THINK MEN WHO HAVE A PIERCED EAR ARE BETTER PREPARED FOR MARRIAGE. THEY'VE EXPERIENCED PAIN AND BOUGHT JEWELRY.

Rita Rudner

KEEP THE
FLAME
BURNING

**ONE SHOULD
ALWAYS BE IN LOVE.
THAT IS THE REASON
ONE SHOULD
NEVER MARRY.**

Oscar Wilde

**A SLIGHT TOUCH OF
FRIENDLY MALICE
AND AMUSEMENT
TOWARDS THOSE
WE LOVE KEEPS
OUR AFFECTIONS
FOR THEM FROM
TURNING FLAT.**

Logan Pearsall Smith

THERE ARE TWO WAYS TO HANDLE A WOMAN, AND NOBODY KNOWS EITHER OF THEM.

Kin Hubbard

DON'T MISTAKE PLEASURE FOR HAPPINESS. THEY ARE A DIFFERENT BREED OF DOG.

Josh Billings

**A SENTIMENTAL
PERSON THINKS
THINGS WILL LAST;
A ROMANTIC PERSON
HOPES AGAINST
HOPE THAT THEY
WON'T.**

F Scott Fitzgerald

**MEN ARE FROM
EARTH. WOMEN
ARE FROM EARTH.
DEAL WITH IT.**

George Carlin

VALENTINE

I DON'T UNDERSTAND
WHY CUPID WAS
CHOSEN TO REPRESENT
VALENTINE'S DAY.
WHEN I THINK ABOUT
ROMANCE, THE LAST
THING ON MY MIND IS
A SHORT, CHUBBY
TODDLER COMING AT
ME WITH A WEAPON.

Anon

BIRDS DO IT,
BEES DO IT ...

**BISEXUALITY
IMMEDIATELY
DOUBLES YOUR
CHANCES FOR
A DATE ON
SATURDAY NIGHT.**

Woody Allen

ANY WOMAN WHO THINKS THE WAY TO A MAN'S HEART IS THROUGH HIS STOMACH IS AIMING ABOUT 10 INCHES TOO HIGH.

Adrienne E Gusoff

LOVE IS NOT THE DYING MOAN OF A DISTANT VIOLIN – IT'S THE TRIUMPHANT TWANG OF A BEDSPRING.

S J Perelman

LOVE IS THE SAME AS LIKE EXCEPT YOU FEEL SEXIER.

Judith Viorst

WHOEVER NAMED IT NECKING IS A POOR JUDGE OF ANATOMY.

Groucho Marx

LOVE IS
BLIND

A MAN IN LOVE
MISTAKES A PIMPLE
FOR A DIMPLE.

Japanese proverb

**LOVE MAY BE BLIND,
BUT IT CAN SURE
FIND ITS WAY
AROUND IN
THE DARK!**

Anon

THE ADVANTAGE OF LOVE AT FIRST SIGHT IS THAT IT DELAYS A SECOND SIGHT.

Natalie Clifford Barney

**LOVE IS THE
DELIGHTFUL
INTERVAL BETWEEN
MEETING A
BEAUTIFUL GIRL
AND DISCOVERING
THAT SHE LOOKS
LIKE A HADDOCK.**

John Barrymore

**SOME PEOPLE ARE
BETTER IMAGINED IN
ONE'S BED THAN
FOUND THERE IN
THE MORNING.**

P J O'Rourke

**BEAUTY IS ALL
VERY WELL AT FIRST
SIGHT; BUT WHO
EVER LOOKS AT IT
WHEN IT HAS BEEN
IN THE HOUSE
THREE DAYS?**

George Bernard Shaw

ROMANCE

ROMANCE IS A LOVE AFFAIR IN OTHER THAN DOMESTIC SURROUNDINGS.

Sir Walter Raleigh

**ROMANCE HAS
BEEN ELEGANTLY
DEFINED AS THE
OFFSPRING OF
FICTION AND LOVE.**

Benjamin Disraeli

IN ORDER TO LOVE SIMPLY, IT IS NECESSARY TO KNOW HOW TO SHOW LOVE.

Dostoyevsky

**NOBODY HAS EVER
MEASURED, EVEN
POETS, HOW MUCH
A HEART CAN HOLD.**

Zelda Fitzgerald

**LOVE DOESN'T MAKE
THE WORLD GO
ROUND, LOVE IS
WHAT MAKES THE
RIDE WORTHWHILE.**

Franklin P Jones

COME LIVE IN MY HEART, AND PAY NO RENT.

Samuel Lover

MORE HELP IS AT HAND...